How to Binder

Understanding Shamanism and Spell Casting

By: Sarah Nelson
9781680322415

Publishers Notes

Disclaimer – Speedy Publishing LLC

This publication is intended to provide helpful and informative material. It is not intended to diagnose, treat, cure, or prevent any health problem or condition, nor is intended to replace the advice of a physician. No action should be taken solely on the contents of this book. Always consult your physician or qualified health-care professional on any matters regarding your health and before adopting any suggestions in this book or drawing inferences from it.

The author and publisher specifically disclaim all responsibility for any liability, loss or risk, personal or otherwise, which is incurred as a consequence, directly or indirectly, from the use or application of any contents of this book.

Any and all product names referenced within this book are the trademarks of their respective owners. None of these owners have sponsored, authorized, endorsed, or approved this book.

Always read all information provided by the manufacturers' product labels before using their products. The author and publisher are not responsible for claims made by manufacturers.

This book was originally printed before 2014. This is an adapted reprint by Speedy Publishing LLC with newly updated content designed to help readers with much more accurate and timely information and data.

Speedy Publishing LLC

40 E Main Street, Newark, Delaware, 19711

Contact Us: 1-888-248-4521

Website: http://www.speedypublishing.co

REPRINTED Paperback Edition: ISBN: 9781680322415

Manufactured in the United States of America

DEDICATION

I dedicate this book to my mother. Thank you for all your love and for believing in me.

TABLE OF CONTENTS

Publishers Notes 2

Dedication 3

Table of Contents 4

Chapter 1- Spell Binding with a Shaman 5

Chapter 2- Spell Binding Through Shamanism 10

Chapter 3- Relationship of Etheogens and Spell Binding 15

Chapter 4- Tools of Shaman for Spell Binding 20

Chapter 5- Shamanism Spell Binding Variations 25

Chapter 6- The True Power of Spell Binding 28

Chapter 7- Spell Binding, Paranormal, Origin 32

Chapter 8- Black and White Spell Binding Magic 39

Chapter 9- Say the Right Spell Binding Words 43

Chapter 10- Spell Binding is not For Everyone 50

Chapter 11- Unleash the Truth of Spell Binding 54

About The Author 57

Chapter 1 - Spell Binding with a Shaman

In various human societies these days, there exist some individuals who job is to supplement those religious practices of other people. These individuals also exist to guide people in such religious practices. These individuals are really skilled at influencing and contacting supernatural beings as well as manipulating some supernatural forces. Such individuals are called Shamans and they are actually practicing what is commonly called Shamanism. Get all the info you need here.

Shamanism is an ancient spiritual belief of the Turkic and Mongolian people living in Siberia, Central Asia and in the far west part of the Easter Europe. In Mongolia and Siberia, this is also usually called "Tengerism" since it also means "honoring of spirits".

The practice of shamanism is not a religion, it is actually a method. This practice coexists with a lot of established religions in various cultures. In Siberia, you will find shamanism that coexist with

Lamaism and Buddhism, and in the country of Japan, it coexist with Buddhism.

It is true that many shamans are mostly in animistic cultures and animism means that individuals believe that spirits exist. It is also important to remember that Shamanism is neither an exclusionary nor a system of faith.

The Basics

Shamanism was actually first recognized by the Western observers who are working among different herding societies in northern and central Asia and it's from the language of one of such societies, Siberia's Tungus-speaking peoples, where the term "shaman" was derived.

The word is "saman" in the Siberian Tungustic which means "one who is raised, excited and moved," and it also refers to persons who, during their a state of trance, are visiting the realm of various mystical beings in order to communicate and interact with them, and during the process, obtain mystical power. So, in the original language of Tungus, shaman refers to an individual who is making a journey to the non-ordinary reality.

The primary functions of shaman who are practicing this method, or shamanism are assisting the dead towards the afterworld, who acts as medium between the dead and the living.

They are also determining from the right kind of medicine to heal their patients from those mystical beings. In some regions, Shamanism does not really involve a power to heal or cure a certain illness, but also determine the cause of the disease of malady.

Many people, especially in the present days do not really know what shamanism means. There are a lot of terms such as sorcerer, witch doctor, witch and even wizard that have their own ambiguities, preconceptions and connotations associated with them. Though the term shaman comes from Siberia, the method or the practice of Shamanism has started to exist in various inhabited continents.

Most of the time, Shamans are also referred as "people who know" or seers in their own tribal languages since they are involved in a particular system of knowledge that is based on firsthand experience. It is import ant to note that Shamanism is not really a belief system.

It is actually based on some personal experiments that are conducted to obtain information, to heal and to do some other things. As a matter of fact, if these shamans do not get results, then they will no longer be used in their tribe by people. If you are wondering how you could recognize if an individual is a shaman, it is actually very simple. Know if they are able to perform miracles and if they journey to the other worlds. Shamanism is also a way of life and a way to connect with the entire creation and the nature.

Function of a Shaman

The social role of a shaman may be defined through a set of interrelated rights, obligations and behaviors as conceptualized by individuals in a certain social circumstance and an expected behavior in an individual in their social position and cultural and social status. Today, there are a lot of misconceptions related to shamans and their roles.

How to Become a Spell Binder
The Roles

Healer

A shaman has various roles in the society. Shamans may actually serve the role of a healer in various shamanic societies. They obtain their knowledge and their power to heal through accessing the world of spirits. They make their journey into the realm of spirits and obtain their knowledge in it. Most of the time, they acquire or has one or more assistant or helper entities in the world of spirits.

These entities are mostly spirits in the form of an animal or spirits of healing plants. Sometimes, such entities are also those who departed shamans or some of their other ancestors.

In their way of healing, they are entering the body of the sick individual in order to confront the spirit that causes the patient to get sick. They heal their patients through banishing that infectious spirit. Also, there are a lot of shamans who are knowledgeable about the plant life within their area. They also use herbal regimen to heal the sick.

Mediator

Shaman also acts as mediators within their culture. Shamans are viewed as individuals who communicate with the some spirits on behalf of their community, which include communicating with the spirits of the dead. In various cultures, their role as mediators can be well illustrated through some of their symbols and objects. Shamans mediate between religious entities and ordinary people.

In some cultured, they are also referred to as seers or soothsayers, astrologers, mediums, palm readers and many other diviners. They have different roles in the society and in some societies; they are able to perform great miracles.

Other Roles of the Shaman

As being practiced by Siberia's Reindeer Tungus, shamans are also those individuals who have amazing power to control some mystic entities such as spirits. They can also prevent such spirits from causing any harm to people and on some occasions, they serve as mediums for spirits.

The Tungus shamans, who can either be men or women, are using some special tools of paraphernalia like tambourines, mirrors, costumes and so many other equipments. As being said, they make journey in the world of spirits and do some function for their individual clients and even groups as a whole. They are also able to find lost objects, determine the cause of one's illness, confer a special power in some conflicts and predict some events in the future.

The primary role of shamans is actually to maintain and restore balance in their community. They are conducting rituals of protections, blessings, divination and hunting magic. They are also curing illnesses with spiritual causes like spiritual pollution, spiritual intrusion, curses and soul souls. Shamans are also referred to as caretakers of the traditional culture. Due to their knowledge with regards to ancient tradition, throughout various ages, their counsel has actually been sought by many people.

Chapter 2- Spell Binding Through Shamanism

Shamans interact with spirits and deities not only through prayer but also through offerings and rituals and by direct contacts with those spirits themselves.

They have also been found in each period of history all over the world and they perform different functions that are essential to the society of community where they belong. There are also some shamanism beliefs that all shamans all over the world hold in common. These core beliefs are really important because these give comfort, wisdom and meaning to many people from the different parts of the world.

One of the most common shamanism beliefs is that everyone and everything is part of a certain pattern and thus, they are all interrelated. Things around us are connected with each other. Shamans also believe that an alternate reality exists. This is often referred to as the dreamtime of the spirit world by the traditional individuals or as no ordinary reality by the modern mystics.

The Beliefs

Shamans likewise believe that some individuals have the ability to obtain the transcendent state of consciousness and to enter the alternate reality for healing of self as well as others and for problem solving. Such belief is mostly accompanied by a powerful and really strong desire to experience personally an alternate reality.

Also, one of the most evident shamanism beliefs is the existence if spirit teachers and helpers who lives in an alternate reality. Though most modern mystics does not tend to affiliate with some organizes religion, they regard Jesus of Nazareth as powerful spirit teacher.

Most of shamans also profess their belief in various forms of supernatural godlike beings and consciousness. Also, for them, everything, both inanimate and animate is imbued with soul or a personal supernatural essence.

Another shamanism common belief relates to the existence of a vital force or an impersonal power that is pervading in many things and is being expressed as a life force in some inanimate beings – the chi of the Chinese, mana of Polynesians, prana of yoga, Baraka of Muslims and the num of Kalahari bushmen.

They also believe that personal energy body exists and it can be perceived by others as an aura. This can also be improved through some energy that centers inside it which is called meridians and chakras in the Eastern thought.

How to Become a Spell Binder

Shamanism is actually base on a principle that our visible world is pervaded by spirits or invisible forces which create great impacts in the lives of human beings. Shamanism also requires special abilities and individualized knowledge and it operates outside those established religions. There are also different variations of shamanism all over the world and some of the most beliefs are also shared by the entire forms of shamani.

A Connection to Everything

In the eyes of a shaman, every child, man and woman has an important connection to his or her family, to other humans, to the entire forms of life and to all the elements in nature which include animals, clouds, plants, winds, rocks, trees, minerals and even the earth as a whole.

The fundamental practice and principle of shamanism is to be able to promote planetary health and individual, spiritual growth, promote relationships and empowerment.

Shamans believe that the world is consisting of two great realities – the non-ordinary and the ordinary. The former is known as the physical world that is bound by time and space, whereas the latter is the invisible spirit world.

The Concepts

Shamans are providing the missing link of connection with the realm of spirits. Because we experience environmental crises today, we really need shamans today more than ever. The world's future and the environment greatly depend upon their beliefs and wisdom.

Shamans learn through their experience and by those teachings provided by other people. The most evident distinguishing factor between some other mystics and healers these days and the Shaman is the journey which is mostly referred to as the "flight of the soul". Through entering an altered consciousness state, Shamans have the ability to journey into non-ordinary world to seek wisdom and guidance from those wise spirits for healing and helping the ordinary world.

The utmost calling of every Shaman is to be able to sustain and reinstate harmony and balance to put an end to worldly suffering and pain. Also, when shamans enter into the other world, they are performing soul retrieval. They are entering a trace state and then go out of one's body in order to hunt down the portions of the essence of the person. If you are able to experience multiple losses of soul in your life, shamans may help you in restoring back your soul.

Shamans believe in the existence of spirits and these play vital roles both in the human society and in an individual. They are able to communicate with the world of spirits and perform healing practices. By entering into the world of spirits, they are also able to retrieve ones soul.

Your soul is actually your essence and it is how your mortal spirit's molecules connect with your physical and conscious forms. However, such connection can always be lost as well as its essence. Such essence is actually conscious and this can always choose to leave because of some situations. This concept is mostly referred to as the soul loss.

When this happens, shamans have the ability to retrieve your lose soul. From the views of shamans, illness mostly leads to loss soul. Also, this happens when there is a breakdown in the relationship

How to Become a Spell Binder
between you and the spirit, as well as the breakdown between the natural world and the person.

In order to retrieve the soul, shamans journey in order to find those missing parts of your souls, be able to negotiate returns and assist you in reintegrating those fragmented piece.

Chapter 3- Relationship of Etheogens and Spell Binding

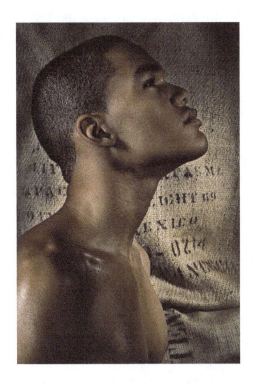

As being said, shamans are passing through the axis mundi and they are entering into the spirit world through effecting transitions of consciousness and entering into an ecstatic trance, which can become successful auto hypnotically or with the use of the entheogens.

If you are wondering about what an entheogen is, well this is actually a psychoactive substance that is being used in shamanic, religious or even in the spiritual context.

Entheogens also have the ability to supplement some diverse practices essential for revelation and transcendence which include psychonautics, psychedelic, meditation and psychedelic therapy, visionary art and magic.

How to Become a Spell Binder
What Is It

Entheogens have actually been used in many ritualized contexts for many years and their religious value is perfectly establishes in modern and anthropological evidence. There are actually several examples of Entheogens which include psilocybin mushrooms, cannabis, peyote, Ipomoea tricolor, Amanita muscaria, ayahuasca, uncured tobacco and Salvia divinorum.

Whether or not in traditional or formal religious structure, Entheogens are valuable psychoactive substances especially when they are used for spiritual and religious effects.

Entheogens are just some of the most important psychoactive drugs that are used by shamans. These are also been used over centuries for various purposes whether medicinal, ritual, spiritual, recreational and others.

This is an essential type of psychoactive drug that is being used not only by shamans by also by some people due to its ability to induce a special type of experience within the conscious mind of a person. This is also one of the valuable tools used by shamans in their journey to the other world.

The use of an entheogen is also found in various healing traditions; this is also due to the great influence of shamans. These psychoactive substances have also been used as an essential tool in order to promote the different types of learning and understanding.

Entheogens have also been used in order to profoundly stimulate some transcendent experiences, and in these days, entheogen has been the main term that is being used for the shamanic inebriants.

Entheogens are essential plant substances and when these are ingested, they will provide an individual a divine experience. In the past, this has been called psychotomimetics and hallucinogens.

Also, these substances are really important because they cause, or even help a person identify with other's feelings or experience a sense of connected with other persons. Because of the very nature of these substances, these have been effectively used when shamans are entering into the spirit world and healing people or retrieving their souls.

Music to Shaman

There are a lot of songs and music related to shamanism. Shamanic songs and music actually include both music that is being used as part of their ritual and practices. The rituals of shamans are actually rituals and not musical performances which shapes musical dimension.

In the practice of shamanism, shamans have even more active musical role as compared to mediums in spirit possession. Shamans are using different ways in order to make sounds and of the sounds they are produced has different purposes. The drumming of shamans and their song particularly is of great importance.

Though all shamans are using drumming as well as singing and other musical instruments, it is important to remember that s shamanic ritual is not actually a musical performance, but rather their music is directed to the spirits instead of offering it to their audience.

How to Become a Spell Binder
The Music

Their ritual performance comprises of series of actions and their attention is always directed towards their visualization of the realm of the spirits. They are also using their songs and music in order to communicate with the spirits. From the musical perspective, the ritual performances performed by shamans have a discontinuity distinctive feature.

There might be breaks that can happen for various reasons. Sometimes, it is due to the difficulty to communicate with the spirit of the shaman requires calling another different spirit. The rhythmic dimension of their music during their rituals has been interrelated to a certain idea of both incorporating the nature's rhythm and then magically rearticulate them.

The songs and music related to shamanism mostly comprises of drumming and instrumental music which are really great for meditation during the present time. These may also serve as very relaxing songs for many individuals. Apart from that, the music and songs of shamans that one can listen to these days are really soothing to the soul.

There are also many shamans who dance and imitate birds and animals. They possess a very striking ability of incarnating and the gift of constant changing their outward and inward appearance.

During their ritual period, they are talking and reciting musically, they are speaking their voice of their spirit assistant, converse with them and they also have the ability to imitate the voice of animals and birds as well as their spirit helper.

The primary characteristic feature in the activities of shamans has a close connection with art and musical art. Shamans are actually singers and guardians. They pass on the art of singing from one generation to others. While listening to the ceremonies of shaman, people also learned ways to intone music, their sound row, as well as their melodies.

If you notice the shamanic songs and music, you can identify that their songs also serve as reflections of their skills, needs, interests, habits and feelings. In shamanic rituals, one can identify the significant within their melodious strength, the lyrical pages in their music, the refinement of their song's language and the beautiful harmony of their musical rhythms.

CHAPTER 4- TOOLS OF SHAMAN FOR SPELL BINDING

In order to perform their rituals, there are many different tools that are being used in shamanism. These tools have been really important for shamans not just in performing their rituals but also in their journey to the world of spirits and when they are performing soul retrieval or healing one's souls.

These souls have been connected with shamans and their practice throughout the years and these have been one of the most essential symbols.

Tools

The Drums – the rhythmic power of drums is compared to the earth's heartbeat and it is also deeply anchored in shamanic practice.

Shamans journey on the every beat of the drum to the world of spirits and then they return with power. The drum, together with rattle is an essential tool of their trade.

Rattles – these are filled with great power and also serve as the power antennae. In various parts of the world, rattles are being used with drums and in the country of Siberia; these are commonly built into the drumstick or drum. These are very easy to carry and they might be just simple tools but they are really are powerful. Rattles have various functions in shamanism; they can be used in some rituals in order to consecrate a sacred place and they are also used to speak as the deity's voice and to heal.

The shaman's mirror – this tool is used by many shamanic practitioners for journeying, energetic protection, healing works and divination. It is a round disc that is also used by many shamans as an essential aid in their healing therapies, together with some other important tools used in shamanism like rattles and drums.

Incense – this tool speaks to one's soul as well as its senses. The smokes that come from this tool both invoke bless and purify ritually. Along with the rattling, singing and drumming, smoke is creating a very powerful ritual. In some shamanic traditions, they are using some different kind of incense to use as an important tool in their rituals.

Flutes – these tools are also used in various shamanism rituals. These are very easy to play. Flutes are also really ideal for helping a shaman shift in consciousness. This kind of instrument is not only used during their rituals, it has also been used when shamans are journeying into the spirit world.

The Staffs – these tools obtain an important role in the practice of shamanism in various cultures, most particularly in Scandinavian magic tradition. This has also been used as a valuable carved record of one's very long journey. It symbolizes authority and it serves as a support and also a weapon.

Orgons – this serves as a very special site for shamans to have a contact with the spirits. It serves as an important site of communicating between the physical world and the spirits. This is also a specially created home spirits.

Orgons are one of the most valuable shaman tools especially in Siberia and Mongolia and in almost the entire tribes that are using them. Orgons come in various forms; they can actually be carved out of a wood, can be painted in leather or even mounted on wooden hoops and be made from metal materials. These also serve as the house of spirits and shamans are passing this from generation to generation since spirits will always live inside them.

Folklore

There are many different myths, legends and folk tales from the different parts of the world. Each country and region has their own stories to tell that reflects their society and the kind of life they live in.

These pieces of literature have been handed down from generation to generation that helped the people of today understand the life of their ancestors and those who once lived in the world.

Shamanism has been practiced all over the world and there are various forms of literatures, especially folk tales that mimic the concept of shamanism. A shaman is often regarded as a spiritually selected individual in touch with the magical and spiritual world, thus it can be concluded that the witches can fall within the realm of shamans.

Also, when the characters killed the witch, the witch then was the one that had experience death. It is important to note that having an experience with death is just another important stage during the initiatory practices of shamanism.

Folk Tales

In various famous folk tales these days, such as "Hanses and Gretel", there are some shamanic initiations which serve as one of the most important hidden themes within the tale. While this tale is mostly recognized as symbolizing a passage rite, there can be seen some underlying elements mimicking the shamanic initiations' universal concept.

Also, one can see various shamanic themes in some Georgian Folktales as well in American Folk tales. A lot of stories in these places revolve around spirituality, the nature of spirits and the person's ability to travel from this world into the world of spirits.

Apart from that, many different forms of literatures, priest and shamans are present. They are performing incantation and rituals in order to heal people and the characters of each tale.

Folk tales, just the same as other forms of literatures have universal truths as their characteristics.

How to Become a Spell Binder

The underlying themes related to shamanism in various folk tales all over the world is just a manifestation that even during the time of our ancestors, or those who are able to narrate these folk tales, the concept of shamanism is already present. The concept of shamanism is actually universal and timely. It was real during those times and its concept is still true today.

CHAPTER 5- SHAMANISM SPELL BINDING VARIATIONS

Shamanism is recognizes as a range of traditional practices and beliefs that are concerned with having a communication with the realm of spirits. There are actually different variations and types of shamans all over the world and they have different functions and perform various rituals.

There are actually three various types of shamans – the Yellow, White and Black. The Black and White shamans are traditional and the Yellow shamans come as the result of the influence from Buddhism.

How to Become a Spell Binder

It's really important to note that the "White" and "Black" designations don't necessarily means good and evil. It just means that they are different spirit types that they are working with. In the Siberian tradition, every direction has a designated color and the color of a shaman is determined from the direction to which he obtains his power.

Variations

Black Shamans – they serve as the most powerful shamans among their type and they obtain their strength and power from Northern direction. They are recognized as warrior shamans and they are able to overcome evil through fighting might versus might. Black shamans are models of discipline and courage.

Based on history, these shamans are able to fulfill their duties in both times of combat or war and in times of peace. During wartime, they are boosting the morale of their soldiers and they are doing ceremonies in order to help in each battle. The army's power was connected to them, so they are always recruited in during wars.

In times of peace, they serve as valuable advisors and they are conducting foreign policy through making alliances and promoting peace. During the Mongolian Empire, the entire treaties were being ratified by the shaman ceremonies.

White Shamans – they obtain their power from Western Direction and due to this, they are directing their prayers towards the Western Heavens. White Shamans have the ability to create good relationships with all the spirits of nature and they are also recognized as spirits of peace.

They provide emphasis on pacifying those angry spirits and focus in helping humans to live a life with a good balance in nature.

They also do blessings and divination, but there is one singe that they can't do, and it is the shaman's curse.

In the Mongol Empire, While Shamans dealt with the local affairs and they were serving the administrators. They are also mostly concerned with the everyday lives of many people.

Yellow Shamans – between the seventeenth and nineteenth centuries, the Tibetan Buddhism or the Lamaism had imposed itself on Mongolian people and during that time, it was really hard for the shamans.

The Black Shamans had started to refuse submitting to foreign religions and the White Shamans have been divided. There were some who submitted to the Buddhist authority and they because the Yellow Shamans. The other White Shamans then refused to surrender their traditions.

Shamanism is still practiced today in various countries. As a matter of fact, this remains as an essential practice in Huns, Altaic people, Uralic as well as in Udmurtia and Mari-El. It is also still being in Korea, particularly in South Korea where their role is usually taken by those women called mudangs and the male shamans are called baksoo mudangs. There are different shamans in every country and in every region and they play a vital role in the society where they belong.

Chapter 6 - The True Power of Spell Binding

Many individuals wish to learn Witchcraft as they believe it's going to be a fast and simple way to rewards. They believe that you follow the instructions to light a candle, state a few words, and whoosh-- stuff happens. It doesn't really happen like that.

Spells don't really work the way you might think-- spells are a bit like recipes. You may attempt to follow along, however if you aren't acquainted with the ingredients, if you don't comprehend the techniques, if you don't have a general understanding of the techniques or practice very much, it will be haphazard.

As a matter of fact, the more you rely on the recipe, without truly learning what makes them work, the more misses you'll get than hits.

The Basics

If you get a recipe at that stage, you don't even understand enough about cooking to know if it's good, or not. If you can't find the precise ingredients, or the correct tool, you aren't truly sure what to do or how it will affect the result of the dish. All you may do is cross your fingers and trust for the best. Even if it turns out good once, you don't understand why so you can't truly repeat it.

You need to get past the stage of using others recipes if you want to truly find out how to cook. You have to learn to comprehend the ingredients, the tools, hone those skills so that you don't have to keep reading someone else's instructions, Then you may accomplish your own vision of a dish, as you've learned what to do.

Witchcraft, like any other skills, calls for more than simply following "recipes"-- or in this case, spells that others write down. It's not enough to simply trust it, follow instructions and trust for the best. It demands that you learn it requires that you become acquainted with the ingredients (components), the tools, the strategies.

Here, I'd like to supply you with some information and give you an overview of the kinds of matters involved.

Practicing casting spells is only enhanced by likewise studying theory. I understand a lot of individuals aren't all that tickled about studying or reading explanations for things, but it truly makes a difference.

As mentioned previously, putting the correct ingredients together provides you haphazard results. Understanding what you're doing and why you're doing it, step-ups your success rate. It helps you comprehend what you're doing on a lot of levels. It's simpler to spot those spells that will work, and those that don't; it's simpler to design your own for your particular purposes. It's simpler to work with your tools and components, the more you learn.

So the reading truly pays off. There are many philosophies when it concerns magic and how it works, which is likewise why it pays to read explanations, theory, philosophies.

The most crucial tool for Witchcraft isn't the cauldron, nor the candle, nor is it even the spell book. It's the brain.

The stronger you are able to make your brain, the better a Witch you will be. It's crucial to learn how to:

• Sustain focus for long time periods

• Move at will from one state of awareness to another

• Get at untapped parts of the conscious and subconscious mind more easily

• Perfect your sensory perceptions

• Control energy (raising, holding, releasing, directing)

The way you beef up your brain is the same way you'd beef up any other muscles-- you have to 'exercise' it.

Believe it or not, general brain teasers and puzzles are a great part of that. Reading is a different really great part to beef up your brain-- think of it as suitable nourishment.

There are likewise psychic exercises* to help you improve your mental abilities. A lot of exercises teach you how to utilize all your senses, as well as your extra-senses. They likewise teach you how to sense and gain command over energy.

Likely the most beneficial way to beef up the brain is the M-word; that's right-- meditation*. I know many individuals do not like that word, and are not patient enough to master the procedure, however meditation for the brain is like weight training for the body.

Bear in mind, meditation is not all about sitting quiet, wiping the brain blank and becoming bored for 60 minutes. There are a lot of different focal points, a lot of meditative strategies, and for those who don't like to sit still there's even moving meditations. If you are going to practice casting spells, you ought to consider at least giving it a try.

Chapter 7- Spell Binding, Paranormal, Origin

Several simply wish to learn how to make things happen to better their lives or fulfill a goal that would not usually be accomplished. It has been broadly believed that spells involved the utilization of these powers to bring harm to individuals of a community or their belongings.

Witches were working with the devil which is why prosecution was typical. Since the mid twentieth century, the term spells has sometimes been explained differently to differentiate between bad spells and good spells.

The concept of spells as adverse is commonly treated as a means of explaining human bad luck by blaming it either on a supernatural entity or a known individual in the community. Several blame their bad luck or "misfortune" on curses and other individuals doing spells against them.

Beliefs in spells scared many individuals for centuries frequently leading to witch hunts where the goal was to apprehend, prosecute and kill anybody who was practicing spells. It didn't matter if the witch was Pagan or Wiccan. Any form of spells or spell casting was viewed as illegal and punishable by demise. Rumors of hexes by the witches that were prosecuted are yet believed to tarry to this day in particular places.

During the 20's covens began to organize in private and documented meetings and cast spells. Studies on spells and rituals went on at this time and a lot of books were released. Writers were hunted down and put behind bars for their writings. What most individuals didn't understand is that the Wiccan and pagan religions were really similar to Christian religion.

They believed in the Christian God, along with Mother Nature. Studies demonstrated that including Mother Nature in their prayers and honoring her regularly rendered positive energy into the world and let them channel that favorable energy into other facets of their focus.

There are a lot of misconceptions about spells. Among them are sacrifices. Authentic witches of the Wiccan and pagan religions will never sacrifice anything a live for the sake of a spell. They don't believe in taking any sort of life for the sake of achieving a goal.

A lot of individuals associate spells and casting spells with wickedness and black magic when that is not what truly goes on. A lot of wiccans and pagan solely practice white magic which is respectful of everybody and brings no harm on anybody or anything.

Meaning of Paranormal

In today's world there's an ever-increasing intrigue with the paranormal with both religious and non-religious individuals. The intrigue appears strongest in those without deep religious convictions, maybe because our society leaves a lot of individuals yearning for something to believe in that is bigger than themselves.

However in recent decades a rising number of earnest Christians likewise have developed an interest in unexplained phenomena. A lot of people have really pronounced feelings about these matters, a few believing wholeheartedly in the validness of paranormal phenomena, other people feeling even as powerfully that all such claims are bogus and that even the investigation of these matters is crazy.

Paranormal nomenclature frequently is ambiguous and may have assorted meanings depending upon the outlook of the individual using the terms. For the purposes of this, we shall define our terms as outlined here.

Paranormal and Other Terms

Paranormal. The American Psychological Association specifies paranormal to mean "any phenomenon that in one or more respects exceeds the limits of what is deemed physically possible according to current scientific assumptions." So, the word "paranormal" is an umbrella term utilized to name a broad range of phenomena running from ESP to the supernatural.

This general definition would include all issues that involve such things as precognition, mind-reading, telekinesis, spirits, devils, angels, occultism, black magic, miracles, and even God. While miracles, angels, and other biblically supported supernatural themes fall inside the realm of the paranormal, here we shall limit the term to refer to more contemporary events like ESP, ghosts and apparitions, poltergeists, magic, and fortune-telling. These are the realms more commonly investigated by modern-day researchers and are not inevitably religion-based suppositions.

The prefix of the term "paranormal" is para, meaning "beyond," and the term therefore describes something that's past the norm or something that doesn't have a normal or natural account for its being or occurrence.

There are a lot of things in our day-to-day lives that at first sight seem to be paranormal, just these issues can't genuinely be classed as paranormal if normal or natural accounts for them may be observed. An issue can't be 'paranormal' unless we may first demonstrate that it is not 'normal. To give an illustration, we all understand what the acronym UFO means — unidentified flying object.

A lot of us have run across flying objects that we couldn't promptly identify. However what becomes of a UFO if we later distinguish it as a sort of experimental aircraft? It's no longer unknown and therefore can't retain the classification of a UFO. In the same fashion, an issue that we might think to be paranormal can't remain a paranormal issue if a normal account for it may be found.

Only those issues that can't be explained by natural means may be classified (at least temporarily) as paranormal, and they remain so only till a natural explanation may be found. So in that sense, "paranormal" becomes only an impermanent designation till the issue may be amply studied and assessed with every means presently known to us.

How to Become a Spell Binder

While technically "supernatural" and "paranormal" have basically the same meanings, they've different connotations. Super means "above" or "beyond," and natural implies that which is in accordance with the rules of nature. Supernatural, then, relates to anything that's beyond the natural or above the natural laws of the cosmos as we comprehend it.

For instance, if an object might levitate (defy the law of gravity), that might be a supernatural happening — provided no natural means might be discovered that would cause the thing to levitate. However this definition likewise includes a lot of things bearing on religion. God is supernatural as He is above the natural laws of the cosmos.

The Incarnation, the Resurrection, miracles, angels, and so forth, likewise are supernatural. All Christians trust in the supernatural. However that doesn't necessarily imply that all Christians trust in everything many individuals claim are supernatural.

The occult has to do not just with the supernatural however likewise with matters that are thought mystical, hidden, or secret. It implies something that may be understood solely by those initiated into particular secrets, like magic.

Commonly included in the realm of the occult are such matters as magic (true magic, not sleight of hand), sorcery, black magic, mediumistic abilities, communication with ghosts, or worship of devils or false gods.

Frequently individuals who practice such matters trust they have the power to do or understand things that normal individuals can't. Voodoo is a form of occultism; holding a séance is an occult practice.

We have to remember that a lot of things in these areas intersect, but, and that this is among the main reasons a lot of people object to Christians becoming involved in any area of para-normal investigation. A few Christians see no difference between holding a séance and exploring telepathic powers.

Even individuals who fully trust in the paranormal and practice paranormal actions themselves occasionally disagree over whether particular phenomena are due to the influence of the occult or are merely natural powers for which we haven't yet discovered natural explanations. For example, we might encounter 2 individuals who both claim to bear precognitive abilities. Not everybody agrees whether clairvoyance ought to be classified as an occult act or merely a psychic power.

A different matter we have to watch with our terminology is the word "magic." As we generally think of it, magic is a cunning means of amusement using assorted slight-of-hand strategies devised to fool the observer's eye. Stage magicians are truly not "magicians" in the genuine sense of the word however are in reality "illusionists." Everything he accomplishes has a natural explanation. What he does is produce an illusion, making it look as though something has occurred that truly hasn't.

True magic is the study of the occult arts. We said that occultism dwells on the mystical and hidden, the things that only the initiated might know. A genuine magician is one who claims to have found out these secrets and may tap into supernatural powers. There are broadly thought to be 3 kinds of magic:

White magic, or magic established on knowledge of the hush-hush things of the Bible and which is based on a belief in God. The term likewise is utilized by some non-Christians to refer to magic that's designed to assist instead of hurt individuals. Some trust that white magic is in fact only black art with a scriptural disguise.

Black magic, or magic broadly based on knowledge of wicked powers. Black magic frequently is practiced by those who worship fiends or Satan. Wiccans (who don't believe in Satan) commonly utilize the term to refer to magic planned to harm instead of assist individuals.

Sympathetic magic. A few think there's a third type of magic named sympathetic magic or natural magic. They claim that this is a sort of magic based on "neutral forces" that are neither white nor black. This sort of magic is frequently discovered in a lot of folk cures like in the practice of twining a black thread around warts while repeating a spell and then placing the thread below a piece of guttering in the trust that this will make the warts go away.

Most individuals who claim to utilize white magic do so for the good of humankind, trusting that they may help other people. Most that practice black magic do so either for personal gain or for wicked intents.

Other terms will be defined as we progress through our study.

Not everybody may agree with the descriptions here, but they're offered in the hope that people will have a better understanding of the paranormal and understand better how to deal with the subject when faced with unusual phenomena.

CHAPTER 8- BLACK AND WHITE SPELL BINDING MAGIC

In ancient times individuals were exceedingly religious minded. With blind faith they trusted in anything they found commodious. They never had a mentality to question and dispute the facts that they were asked to trust in.

They began worshiping nature and its forces. This was great in one way as in the process they attempted to preserve it and not upset the natural balance.

The Black Arts

However at the same time this unquestionable belief wasn't free from flaws. They began depending upon the energy of spirits and black magic. They trusted this to be a force in front of whose wrath they had to fall helplessly. This unconditional faith was something individuals of the primitive ages could not help.

How to Become a Spell Binder

However this isn't the case in the contemporary world. You may definitely comprehend the forces governing the black magic spell rituals. After that, it's completely up to your discretion whether you shall believe in its occult power or not.

The birthplace of black magic is Africa. The word black magic brings up a sense of darkness, and evil and with it affiliated rights and rituals to please power holders of this cosmos. Among the crucial accessories of black magic are the voodoo dolls. It's believed that a lot of powers related to the Devil are affiliated with them which work by activating the powers of human mind.

There are particular concepts of positive and damaging energy, which are present everyplace around us. Black magic spells work with the negative energies to manifest desired changes in your world. It encourages necromancy.

In the Middle East black magicians wanted the blood of beasts and new borns as offerings, which is among the reasons why it wasn't a much opted path. It was one of the critical reasons why using black magic was as bad as perpetrating a crime. The staunch believers thought that the Devil would go down to earth and offer his blessings and satisfy wishes, once anybody could please him with these acts.

There are quite a number of sorts of black magic. A few of them being: thaumaturgy, divination, compassionate embodiment and so forth. Thaumaturgy was thought to have the powers to cure an individual of any disease. All the additional forms are believed to be vested with the power to intrude into natural forces and manipulate it to bring any sort of change one wished for.

All the energies with which black magic worked had something to do with damaging energy collection. It proved really destructive in certain cases for the individual who performed it, because of being careless when dealing with negative energies there are chances that the individual himself gets hit by it.

So be sensible and intelligent while dealing with such forces of the brain.

White Magic Spell Binding

White magic is most generally thought of as healing magic, or spells and rituals that aid individuals. White magic, healing or "good", as contrary to Black magic. True White Magic Spells that work may be utilized to protect, bless, heal, and help yourself or other people.

They may be utilized to bless or purify new ventures, clear and heal the brain and body, shield individuals and places from hexes and curses, turn back wicked magic spells and incantations, reverse foul situations, break jinxes, and allow good dreams and wishes to be granted.

True White Magic Spells that work are all meant to be favorable, uplifting, kind, advantageous, and gentle. White Magic Spells are planned to be defensive, helpful--never injurious. The forms and factors of black magic spells are unlike white magic.

They frequently reflect the focus, aims, or interests of those casting the spells, which is in blunt contrast to the casting of white magic spells. The casting of black magic spells frequently comprises symbolism of those things which could be interpreted as potentially risky or harmful to humans, like sharp, pointed, caustic, and/or hot elements blended with personal objects from the spell's focus (a curl of hair, a drop or blot of blood, personal mementos, and so forth.). And while this distinction is mainly observable in folk magic, it may pertain to additional forms of magic likewise.

How to Become a Spell Binder

Function of white magic-

White magic spells are frequently spells that will better beauty, heal sicknesses, increase luck, and shift the weather to produce sunny days, protect a house or individual, banish wickedness and hold devils at bay.

Practitioners—

Those who practice white magic frequently refer to themselves as priestess, priests, clerics, shamans and witches.

Characteristics of white magic-

White magic spells frequently contain a component that includes talismans or amulets in the casting.

Chapter 9- Say the Right Spell Binding Words

The execution of magic almost always requires the utilization of language. Whether spoken aloud or unspoken, words are oftentimes utilized to access or guide magic power. The association between language and magic is due to a belief in the innate power of words to influence the universe.

This notion is an extension of man's basic utilization of language to describe his environment, in which "the knowledge of the correct words, suitable phrases and the more developed forms of speech, gives man mightiness over and above his own confined field of personal action."

Magic speech is consequently a ritual act and is of equal or even bigger importance to the performance of magic than non-verbal acts.

The Words

Not all speech is considered magic. Only particular words and phrases or words uttered in a particular context are thought to have magic power. Magic language is distinct from scientific language because it's emotive and it changes words into symbols for emotions; whereas in scientific language words are attached to particular meanings and refer to an objective outside reality. Magic language is consequently especially adept at building metaphors that launch symbols and link magic rituals to the world.

The language of magic is sacred, set and utilized for a totally different purpose to that of average life. The 2 forms of language are distinguished through word choice, grammar, style, or by the utilization of particular phrases or forms: prayers, spells, songs, blessings, or chants, for instance. Sacred modes of language frequently use archaic words and forms in an effort to invoke the purity or "truth" of a religious or a cultural "golden age".

A different likely source of the power of words is their secrecy and exclusivity. A great deal of sacred language is separated enough from common language that it's inexplicable to the majority of the population and it may only be utilized and translated by specialized practicians (magicians, priests, shamans, even mullahs).in that respect, Magic languages breach the basic function of language: communication. Yet adherents of magic are yet able to utilize and to value the magic function of words by trusting in the built-in power of the words themselves and in the meaning that they have to supply for those who do comprehend them.

An incantation or enchantment is a charm or spell produced using words. An incantation might take place during a ritual, either a hymn or prayer, and might invoke or praise a deity. In magic, occultism, and witchcraft it's utilized with the intention of casting a spell on an object or an individual and might employ the utilization of pharmakeia. The term derives from Latin "incantare" (tr.), meaning "to chant (a magic spell) upon," from in- "into, upon" and cantare "to sing".

In medieval literature, folklore, fairy tales and modern fantasy fiction, enchantments are charms or spells. The term was loaned into English since around AD 1300. The comparable native English term is "galdor" "song, spell". It has led to the words "enchanter" and "enchantress", for those who utilize enchantments.

Here's an example:

Sweet Dreams Spell

"Feather light on starry night, cozy warm and tired, pleasant dreams and sweetest thoughts as little angels smile."

'Magic', in its simplest form, has been utilized by indigenous cultures to control the surroundings, and bend forces of nature to the will of the user. The Prehistoric man was a great deal in tune with how they were ordered in nature, and frequently felt they had to do sacrifices and offerings to their Gods in order to keep them pleased. These rites are the earliest sorts of spell casting, as their power of giving thanks assisted them in their jobs of farming or accumulating food.

How to Become a Spell Binder
In The Early Days

African and Native American cultures had their Magi and women to perform their spells for like reasons. They utilized wands and crystals to help them in their spell casting, and provided gifts of thanks for the spiritual energies. They centered more on charms and trinkets, or dolls to be carried around, and could perform spells where they were required. Those who performed the spells were extremely revered in their society, as they had demonstrated themselves mighty enough to handle the energy of the spirits.

Egyptian and Greeks were more direct in their spell casting, with their magic being utilized to control the will of others, or giving healing spells direct to a person through their sleep. The performance of the rituals had little change from earlier times, as they still believed that their Gods and Goddesses wished cleanliness from the user, and offerings or gifts in order to say thank you for the utilize of their energies.

All the same, the rise of Christianity during Roman times paved the way for additional sorts of spell casting, lapsing back to the prayers to God, or the utilization of prayer beads and the cross. As the utilization of magic started to be criminalized for their pagan roots, the easy spells presented by the Romans gave them the peace to actively co- exist with additional spell casters from additional cultures for a set time. If the prayers worked, then they'd be given permission to put down their edition of the hereafter and their sort of spells worked for them.

In the middle Ages, the practice of witchery was illegal, and a lot of individuals fell under the governing bodies for the accusation of casting spells on other people.

Stories around these times frequently tell of spells that induced diabolical images to come up in the dreams of the victim, or spells that could shift the temperature of the individual, or evil sorcery that induced the death of an individual.

While it was a crime for spells to be utilized, those who followed the older path were forced underground, and the practice of spells continued.

The nature of these spells was the same as their roots. Little rituals to give thanks for their goods, prayers to their roots, and likewise the utilization of herbs to cure illnesses were utilized in their daily lives until the re-emergence of the pagan religion.

There are a lot of different sorts of spell casting. Each depends upon the cultural backgrounds of the individual requesting assistance. Although the love spell is the most basic, the utilization of spells is exceedingly helpful in supplying the guidance we have in our daily lives.

A prayer, put up to the spirits or to the Gods or Goddesses of your religion is the easiest form of a spell. In asking those of a higher power for help and guidance, the follower is victimization the magical powers of the gods to benefit their lives. But, due to its rigorous religious connotations, it's seldom classed as a spell, but more a way of thanking your opted deity.

Modern Uses of Spell Casting

Due to the fear of persecution, the utilization of spells isn't widely advertised or published, though a few groups are making great efforts to take the dread out of spell casting. An individual might decide to cast spells on their own, and not join a coven, a.k.a. group of individuals who gather together to work on spells and

How to Become a Spell Binder

crafts. An individual who does good spells is likewise called a white witch, for they intend to do great things.

Today

The solitary white witch, a.k.a. your next-door-neighbor, or the individual on the bus, who rehearses spells, may not want everybody to know out of fear of persecution or additional forms of rejection. What may this individual do? How may they exercise magic and do spells with other people around them or at his or her house? Easy.

It is not required that an individual let the Earth know that they're a witch, this is personal preference. An individual might have a nice setting of 3 candles, with a few gems, and perhaps a bowl of water.

To the unknowing individual, this might seem as an innocent ornament.

To the spell caster, this is a place to shine and gather power or to do easy spells.

That lucky charm an individual carries is likewise a spell for good luck, though it wouldn't be though that way. A lucky shirt that a baseball player wears to every game; is a spell. To take the fear out of spells, an individual has to comprehend how spells are done in the contemporary world, or how they're hidden, or masked.

A witch may frequently find what is needed for a spell in the food market. Salt for instance, any salt will do, but sea salt is more pure. Sea salt may be generally found in a lot of stores. Sea salt is likewise utilized to protect against bad energy. Have you ever thrown salt over your shoulder for fortune? You just did spell casting.

Camphor is believed to work very well to clear ones head and help them feel good. Camphor is utilized in magic spell casting much the same way. It's utilized to clear the brain and soul, and a lot more uses. There are a lot of apples and cinnamon scented air sprays, candles and potpourri on the market. Apple and cinnamon are utilized in magical spells to better happiness in the house.

An individual may buy these at a store, wish it in his or her mind to bring about such serenity, and he or she has simply rehearsed a spell. Spell casting may be as simple as an individual needs it to be, or as hard as an individual wants it to be. Casting spells isn't wrong unless the caster makes it wrong.

An individual shouldn't seek out to do injury to other people. The Wiccan Rede states, "An as ye harm none, do what ye will"

CHAPTER 10- SPELL BINDING IS NOT FOR EVERYONE

If you make a spell or ritual, eventually you'll wish to cast it. There are plenty of individuals who cast spells daily. A few are Pagan and others are from an assortment of different religions.

Wicca believes that everything you do will return threefold stronger. If you send out favorable energy with your spells, eventually you'll get favorable energy in response. This is true for damaging energy also. So, prior to casting that spells to give your foe a boil in an uncomfortable place, think! Is it truly worth it? Generally it isn't.

Ethics in spell production are crucial considerations. Before any spell is produced, you have to consider the spells implications. There truly are just 2 rules for spell crafting and they're to do no harm and to not remove somebody's free will. So, ponder before you put pen to paper!

Think First

A different thing to bear in mind is whether you truly need to utilize magic. It's easy to begin casting spells and carrying on rituals for every little thing. Magic is mighty however it's not always necessary or the most beneficial alternative. Frequently spells work in unforeseen ways. They may likewise work less quickly than we'd like or have intriguing side effects.

Magic may likewise make a set of circumstances more complicated. First brainstorm and work out everyday solutions to your issue. Typically it takes less time and less energy to follow through with the routine solutions. Magic isn't a panacea. The caster has to take an active role.

For instance, if you do a spell for successfulness, then don't expect cash to appear in your billfold or purse. You shouldn't continue spending your cash and doing the things you understand are not conducive to prosperity. That simply defeats the purpose of the spell. Rather produce a situation that may capitalize on your spell. Nor should you believe that because you did a spell that it will automatically work out. There are a lot of reasons why spells don't work. Even the most experienced of people cast spells that don't work.

- I don't suggest will binding spells, unless you're willing to take on the karma.

- I don't suggest spells that will hurt individuals unless you're willing to take on karma.

- I don't suggest any personal gain spells, however rather spells that will help you accomplish the means, however not give them to you with no work.

How to Become a Spell Binder

You need a job, so you say that you'll do a job spell. Before you even consider casting attempt all routine aspects to find that job. If you do a job spell, think that somebody else could need it more. A man with a wife and 3 kids who's struggling to make ends meet is competing with you for a job. You cast a job spell, and you receive the job. He's evicted from his house, his loved ones starve and his youngsters can't go to school. Consider the ramifications before you cast.

If you actually decide to cast, make certain you harm none, don't change freewill and don't do a lot of personal gain. If you've almost completed the spell, add a couple of lines that make certain it's for the good of all, harms none, won't have any awful effects and so forth, after all, it's your karma.

Remember:

Ask yourself these questions before you choose to cast a spell:

Have I done everything I may to solve the set of circumstances without magic?

Attempt all the routine methods of getting your goals before resorting to spells. If you want a job, send your resume prior to breaking out the green candles and patchouli. If you're having a dispute with somebody at work, attempt speaking to them about the issue before you go consulting binding spells. That way, you may make sure that your intentions are good.

Will this spell hurt another, or turn somebody's will to mine?

Witches don't cast spells meant to hurt somebody else. Nor do they cast spells on others without their permission, regardless how good their intentions. There's a great reason for this: injurious and meddling spells have an awful tendency to backfire on the individuals who cast them.

If you're watching somebody close to you suffering, it may be hard to think about the situation objectively. If possible, talk over the matter with another trusted pagan acquaintance.

Am I ready to accept the ramifications of this spell, whatever they may be?

Think long and hard about this one. As I've stated previously, you could cast a spell with the greatest of intentions, however wind up with unforeseen ramifications. Meditate a bit on it before you choose to cast the spell. Talk to other witches and see if there isn't a better answer.

Either way, your spell has a better possibility of success if you totally "own" it, and anything that comes from it. The most beneficial way to prevent unexpected ramifications is to follow the guidelines set out above - and, above all, to cast the spell with love in your heart. Making magic is a mighty and transformative experience. You become the subject, and you become the result.

Make certain that what you're requesting is something you'd like to become.

Chapter 11 - Unleash the Truth of Spell Binding

Do spells truly work? Many people say spells are just bunk... and there are people who truly believe.

My brief answer is, "yep". The long answer starts here....

Does It Work

Magic spells don't work the way most individuals "believe" or "wish" they worked.

For instance, you won't cast a love spell and have the person of your dreams knocking at your door a couple of minutes later.

Magic isn't a "magic pill" that will immediately solve all your issues, and get all your desires immediately.

That being stated... Magic does work, and it may alter your life. Here's how...

First recognize that magic is a way to "engage" the power of your brain, spirit, soul, and subconscious mind. When you do it right, not only does it arouse the power of positive thinking in your mind... but it produces a subconscious drive to accomplish what you want. Yes...there are mysterious forces at work in the universe that may help the spell get the effect you want... but even more potent is what occurs inside of you.

To do this...to cast a successful spell calls for just five things. If you "get this right" there's no end to what you may achieve with magic.

It's crucial to allow yourself to feel full emotion for the desire you're attempting to attract. The more emotion you feel and expand into the spell, the better your results. Do whatever you have to do in order to bring up your strongest emotions.

You have to trust in magic with all your heart... even more you have to trust that the spell you're going to cast will help you accomplish the results you want.

You have to stay centered on only the single desire at hand. I never suggest attempting to cast a spell to satisfy more than 1 hope at a time. You have to center on 1 thing and 1 thing only during your spell.

When you cast a spell, don't sit around "waiting" for it to bring in results. You have to begin taking true action on your own that will bring you closer to the goal or want. If you cast a love spell, for instance, get out of the house...make an attempt to smile and engage individuals. Give the spell a chance to work!

Don't obsess on "when" the spell will bring in results... or how speedily things will begin to change. It's best for you to merely forget about the spell, and go on with your life in a positive way. If

How to Become a Spell Binder

you go on to think, think, think, you'll hold back some of the power from the spell.

Spell casting works in a like way as "positive thinking"... and "favorable action". The brain and spirit are really potent tools. Spell casting is merely a way to program these tools to help draw in desires and goals.

Any time you blend favorable thought, belief in yourself, and positive action, you'll succeed in accomplishing what you seek. Spell casting is a fun and empowering way to produce this process inside of you.

About The Author

Sarah Nelson has a great imagination as a kid. She did not stop exploring things; she did not stop asking questions and for that she did not stop looking for answers. Sarah believes that life is so boring if you will only rely on what the eyes can see. She then studied theology and researched more about paranormal activity.

Sarah lives in Georgia with her family where she still continues her quest for more paranormal information.

www.ingramcontent.com/pod-product-compliance
Lightning Source LLC
LaVergne TN
LVHW011044190225
804088LV00011B/720